Teddy Horsley Books for Yo

Light

Teddy Horsley celebrat

by Leslie J. Francis and Nicola M. Slee

Pictures by Ferelith Eccles Williams

COLLINS

The Teddy Horsley series is designed to build bridges between the young child's day to day experiences of the world and the major themes of the Christian year and the Church's worship.

In *Lights*, Teddy Horsley's wonder and awe at the different lights of Christmas help him to share in the Church's celebration of the birth of Christ, the coming of the Light into the world.

'The true light that enlightens every man was coming into the world' (John 1:9).

Collins Liturgical Publications
8 Grafton St, London W1X 3LA

Collins Liturgical Australia
PO Box 3023 Sydney 2001

ISBN 0 00 599866 2

First published 1985

Origination Tien Wah Press Singapore
Made and printed in Great Britain
by Henry Stone & Son (Printers) Ltd.

Teddy Horsley runs to see the lights of Christmas.

He goes into town to see the Christmas decorations

with Mr and Mrs Henry, Lucy, Walter and Betsy Bear.

He gazes at the lights flashing in shop windows.

He laughs at the banners sparkling in the streets.

He warms his paws by the fire in the market place

and dances to the colourful lights in the square.

He is dazzled by the bright flood lights on the town hall

and welcomed by the soft lamps in the cafe.

He points up at the star gleaming high on the tree.

He kneels down to see the lights
streaming through the branches.

Teddy Horsley is glad to see the lights of Christmas.

Teddy Horsley runs to see the lights of Christmas.

He goes into church to see the Christmas crib

with Mr and Mrs Henry, Lucy, Walter and Betsy Bear.

He warms his paws by the shepherds' fire

and dances to the light of the shepherds' lanterns.

He is dazzled by the bright angels in the sky

and welcomed by the soft lamps at the inn.

He points up at the star gleaming over the stable.

He kneels down to see the light
streaming from the manger.

Teddy Horsley is glad to see the Light of Christmas.